Letters, To Women Like Me

Mirtha Michelle Castro Mármol

ALSO BY MIRTHA MICHELLE CASTRO MÁRMOL

Letters, To The Men I Have Loved

Elusive Loves; Amores Esquivos

Letters, To Women Like Me

Contents

Women like me

Studied Cleopatra
Read Plutarch
Just to understand her appeal.
We discovered that it wasn't her features,
Or the way she kohl-lined her eyes.
The power of her thoughts
Was truly her sass.

Women like me

Tend to stay quiet
Until the right time to attack.
We know about battles
And confront loss with pride.
We are infatuated with warriors
We fall in love with their scars.

Women like me

Are always searching for sight
In a world blinded by lights.
We walk with fervor in our eyes
Affirmations in our mouths.
Passions on top of passions
Surviving in our beat up hearts.

Women like me

Are treasures without chests.
We know about love
Beyond ideologies
And beauty,
Beyond our own poetic words.
We exist between spaces
Leaving a trail wherever we go.

Letters, To Women Like Me

Dear Woman Like Me,

One of my least favorite things is running into people I haven't seen in a long time. Especially if they are the–*my life is perfect, I married the perfect guy, my kids only cry when hungry and I eat pizza all the time and have no cellulite* types. First of all, every woman has cellulite. Second of all, no one marries *the perfect guy*–because perfect doesn't exist! That's why I avoid going to places where I know I will run into people who have nothing better to do other than be nosey in regards to what I'm doing with *MY LIFE*. But to my luck I run into people I haven't seen in a long time *all the time.*

"Are you seeing anyone? She asked.

"Not anyone serious" I replied.

Then she spoke the words single people dread to hear:

"I should introduce you to my [SINGLE] friend!

And I replied with my usual response: "Does he have a job?"

(Don't laugh, unemployment is a serious issue that I'm not trying to tackle in anyone's life)

"He's actually very successful" She said.

"*Is he fat?*" I joked.

She laughed and said: "No, he's not, he's actually in great shape"

4

"Cool…Well…*Maybe* we should all get together then." I reluctantly replied.

Most of the time they never catch the word *MAYBE* and actually follow up to set me up with their [SINGLE] friend, and many times I've complied and gone on pointless dates that 80% of the time has only led me to wasting precious time I could've spent doing useful things like watching *ANCIENT ALIENS* on The History Channel or another night out with my AMAZING friends. Because single people *can* do these things. Single people have no one breathing over their necks questioning their TV taste and why they came home too late or too *early*. They don't have to worry about the toilet seat left up or picking up after anyone or waking up to nurse a crying baby. Being single is *A LUXURY* and NOT a disease. In my case, I know that eventually I'll get married and have adorable babies to call my own and I'll spend the rest of my life doing all those other things *married people do*, but why should I rush into trying to find my *perfect match*? Being single is a journey that should be lived. Why is it that in our society being single, is perceived by many as a failure?

When my last long term relationship ended, I felt my life was in shambles. My heart was broken due partly because my mind kept telling my overachieving self that I was a failure. In my mind I had failed at staying in a relationship with a man who I loved and sacrificed so much for. At the time I didn't understand the purpose behind that separation. I didn't understand that it wasn't a failure and that it would turn into one of my biggest blessings. Not because my life became better without him, but because that pain took me on a rollercoaster journey where I established the most important relationship I have: **THE RELATIONSHIP WITH MYSELF.**

For centuries human beings have raised generations with the misconception that another individual can complete us. That another *imperfect* individual can heal us from our brokenness, rescue us from our shame and prevent us from self-destructing. We have given so much power to others over our own lives that we have forgotten the power that lies within each of us, because it's simple: Sometimes loving someone else is easier than loving ourselves. In our daily lives most of us break ourselves down instead of building ourselves up. We dissect our imperfections instead of accepting them as unique qualities. So when a person comes along who makes us feel they love us even when we look crazy in the mornings it creates a false sense of belonging and acceptance. We begin to feel we want to be next to that person at all times because we feel better, prettier, happier, and we feel *complete*. It's romantic, right? As beautiful and poetic as the idea of another person completing us may sound it can be a recipe for disaster. Life itself is not all rose petals, there are thorns too. The honeymoon phase doesn't last forever and becoming dependent on another human being will cause identity issues down the road. The truth is that every individual has the power to heal from within, and better themselves enough to feel whole. The purpose of relationships whether romantic or platonic is to help reveal our own truths as an individual. As a poet this realization was quite harsh for me considering that most of my life I have idealized the concept of romantic love. Throughout my journey of being single I've understood that although the idea of another person completing us is romantic and ravishing, it is the decision that we make to love ourselves that eventually completes us.

I understand the concept of learning to love yourself sounds easier said than done. Perhaps, because not everyone is taught how to love oneself growing up. Many of our parents are probably the product of other people who didn't know how to love themselves either. Thankfully you are your own person and every decision you make today can impact your tomorrow. Years ago when I found myself single, completely alone and having to press re-start on my life–*you know the life I had before him*–I had so many questions and few answers. My inquisitive nature has always believed in the power of questions. After all our circumstances will only change when we begin to question them. True change begins with a question. Revolutions start with a question. Although my life seemed as if it had fallen apart I made the conscious decision to revolutionize my life and not conform to my heartbreak, sadness and what I deemed at the time as a failure. *If anything my error was committing to someone before I knew myself.* To get back on track I needed to commit to myself. I needed to go on a self-discovery journey because the years I had spent in that relationship indeed changed me. We are constantly evolving and the people we surround ourselves with can influence our changes. I no longer was the girl I was before him, so the first question I asked myself was: **WHO AM I?**

It was a scary thing to ask myself that. Can you imagine? I'm a perfectionist, and the Capricorn in me brought up all my negatives before my positives, but that first question of "Who am I?" opened the most amazing can of worms ever! I began to ask myself all the questions I would ask any person I was interested in getting to know. For example, I asked myself: "Mirtha, why do you dress in black so much?" and then I'd answer: "Well, because it's elegant, it's easy, and I'm drawn to it." Then I'd follow up with another question: "Why are you drawn to it?" and I'd answer: "I'm drawn to it because I admit I have a dark side, I like the way it makes me feel when I see it, the color black shouts out mystery and power." With those simple questions on the color black I was able to learn details of my affinity towards that color. If someone now were to ask me why I love black, then I know exactly what to respond. I know some of you might be thinking *"Is this chick schizo?"* All jokes aside I continued to ask myself every question I could think of and that resulted in me **LEARNING WHO I AM.**

Learning who you are takes work and time, but it will be worthwhile. I learned myself so well that it created the confidence I lacked in different areas of my life. No other imperfect human being outside of me had the power to tell me; who I am, what I deserved, what I liked, or what I didn't like and that process resulted in me **ACCEPTING ALL OF ME.** I began to accept my personality flaws, my past, my habits, my body shape, my double jointed fingers, my height, because guess what? At 32 I am not growing any taller! I needed to accept how I was made, how God designed me and see the beauty in me regardless of other people's opinion of me. I transformed the negative thoughts I had about myself into positive ones, because it's all in the mind. I realized that accepting me for who I am was the glue I needed to piece myself back together after experiencing heartbreak. I no longer sought out validation in strangers, relatives, friends or the men that entered my life. Just like we're able to fall in love with another individual after getting to know them, I took the time to know myself. When I entered an honest relationship with myself, I began to *fall in love with me.* By no means am I saying you should only love yourself and be alone for the rest of your life. I don't believe God created us or intended for us to walk alone. I think the relationship we have with others is essential to our human journey and can be a great add on to the relationship we have with ourselves. I believe we should strive to have it all but with an understanding that a fulfilling life truly begins when we learn to love ourselves. You must be whole on your own in order to properly give to others.

The journey of my many questions led me to reflect on my views on different topics such as my career, relationships, love, sex and life in our present world. A world that is rapidly shifting from old ideologies to new traditions. A world in which gender, race and sexuality issues are finally being tackled. A world in which the term "career woman" no longer necessarily means "child-less" and being "child-less" doesn't make you any less of a woman. A world in which independent doesn't signify lonely. A world in which women buy vibrators and aren't afraid to teach men *how* to please them. A world in which more and more people are understanding that equality is a birth right not a special privilege. A world in which the oppressed are becoming militant. A world in which women are learning they have a voice and they aren't afraid to use it. A world in which at the end of the day pain is inevitable, but thankfully there is beauty found in tragedy. For tragedy has the power to motivate the human mind. It can turn weaknesses into strengths and become greatness. Why would you focus on the storm, when you can focus on the rainbow?

I present you *Letters, To Women Like Me,* a compilation of letters and poems all inspired by when I entered the empowering age of 30. An age in which in an old world mentality signified the end of your life as you know it, but luckily in our present world it means quite the opposite. It means an age in which *I finally know myself and I am able to embark on my best life yet.* A life in which I don't know the ending to, but I choose to live the questions and seek the answers and write them along the way. I pray that my words spark your own questions, which I'm confident will lead you to growth. I pray you'll be empowered by the answers you find and I have faith that in that process you will learn to be proud and love the woman you are today, and realize you can take charge and *manifest* the life you want to live.

Genuinely,

Mirtha Michelle Castro Mármol

I AM

If everything I am destined to be
already exists within me.
If my core is made up of tiny molecules
that were once part of something bigger.
Then I must extract
from what I was already given to me
and learn to **BE.**

What Do We Have to Show for after a FAILED Relationship?

She is beautiful. No small town beauty. Her hair is long, naturally long. She has beautiful lashes and perfect cheekbones. She continuously implies she needs a nose job, but the truth is that I think her nose fits perfectly with her face. She works out, and because she's disciplined she has legs any woman could envy. Then she has a smile embodied by straight sparkly teeth, a smile that lights a room, because that's how powerful her presence is. She is what you call an anomaly. She is a woman who is naturally gorgeous, possesses style and is loyal. She is a true gem. That diamond of a woman is my friend and that same woman who is a goddess in many men's eyes was standing in front of me regretting the last seven years of her life.

She had broken up with her longtime love for the millionth time and she said that this time was "*For Real*". She goes on to say she had given him the best years of her life. She was now 27 years old, single and according to her all she had to show for the relationship that ripped her from her youth was a *CELINE BAG*. I tried to cheer her up by telling her it's a great handbag and she can have it for a very long time. It wasn't the time for jokes nor did she care because she had done the math. It was seven years of

14

loving, supporting, cooking, cleaning a very large home, oh and dealing with his annoying assistant. *Yes, she wanted a reimbursement.* I looked at her knowing very well how she felt because at a certain time in my life I also wanted a reimbursement. I asked myself: *Was this the life we intended to live when we fell in love? No!* That was not the life we dreamed of. We wanted more but we fell in love with men that weren't quite ready. Now what did we have to show for it? In her case it was a Celine Bag, but what about the rest of us? We take our time to build these men. We help nurture their talents, their ego and plant the seed to only witness another woman come in and enjoy the fruit of our labor. As she rambled on about how he would never change and the things her heart desired, she said something that overpowered everything else that came out of her mouth. She shouted, **"I taught him how to love!"** I would have hugged her but she was moving around the room at a very rapid pace. I wanted to hug her and congratulate her on finding the gift women are implanted with but sometimes it takes heartbreak to find. *We have the key to love.* We are gifted with the ability to birth, nurture, and with that we are given the key to love! When a woman truly loves she loves differently than a man. Her love can cause change, inspire, transform. Although, she believed her ex would never change, the truth is that most likely he would.

Most likely, he was now going to be different for the next woman in his life. When I was able to get a word in, I told her that he would always think of her because of all the truth she left in him. In the end, all those years of their relationship made him into a better version of himself. Life is one big cycle and if we're lucky, we meet people who help us improve the current version of ourselves. Now that's never the part anyone wants to hear while experiencing the aftermath of a failed relationship. So, after I said that I also told her: *Don't worry your next man will be amazing and more established than your ex!* She smiled and I smiled too because I believed the same for me. You see, that *next* man will be amazing because he would have already been polished, nurtured, and taught how to love by a woman just like me. A woman who like my friend and I perhaps at one point also wanted a reimbursement. Hopefully, that woman also realized that through that failed relationship she had also found her gift–*the key to love because she was a vessel of love.* A gift that will last forever, *way longer* than any Celine bag!

Jaded Girl

"I'm jaded" she said
She gave love and it drifted away–
"I'm jaded" she said.
She was loyal and he went astray–
I wanted to wipe the tears
From her face.
Call her pretty,
And hug her to the point
She felt loved again.
Instead I looked at her
deep in her eyes
And told her being jaded means hope.
From the bottom,
One can only go up!
Women like her
Can rule the world,
Just like the flower
who from concrete rose.
Bravely take that pain,
And turn it into gold.

Tragically in Love

I embraced every single one of your flaws,
as if they were my own.
I dwelled in you and with you,
like two lost peas in a pod.
I curbed with you and for you,
at any given moment.
Our souls if broken down,
were composed by the same particles.
The universe,
had conspired for us,
and with us.
We were madly,
and tragically in love,
at some point in time.

Letters, To Women Like Me

Perfect on Paper or Perfectly Flawed?

He is handsome, very handsome. He is smart, very smart. He is successful, very successful. He is sweet, very sweet. So sweet that when he has you in front of him, I can guarantee he will make you feel as if you're destined for each other. He always says the right things. Not only does he stroke your ego as a woman, but he's also motivational, and inspirational. He makes you want to be better than your already amazing self. So, you begin to walk around on cloud nine and thanking God all at once. All the drama with the previous men was worth it, because you have now found your right match. Oh, and when you guys made love it was intense; beautiful, romantic and magical. In that moment, you deleted every other optional male from your phone, and in your head you began to build your amazing new life with your new man *because that's what women do.* We start falling in love with the idea and start overlooking all the red flags. Now, when do we stop and read into things? When do we start figuring out that what seems to be perfect on paper can actually be flawed?

One night I went out for drinks to celebrate a friend's birthday. We went to Soho House in West Hollywood, which is the usual hang out for most of the celebrities that visit or are residents of LA. No one is star struck, pictures aren't allowed except for the infamous photo booth in the hallway between the two main rooms, and in my opinion it has the best *eastern standard* in the city. When I'm not drinking wine or champagne *that* is my cocktail of choice. A group of us were seated at a big table by the bar area, when my girlfriend points out that a very cute guy kept on staring at me. I realized he's not just a regular cute guy. It was the same cute actor from a TV show I watched for two seasons, and I swear I only watched the second season because of how hot *he* was. I glanced over and indeed he was staring at me. He gave me one of those smiles that left me thinking *"I knew my ass looked amazing in this leather skirt"*. So as I attempt to play coy, and as I feel his eyes and his friend's eyes hovering over me, my girlfriend asked me: "So are you seeing anyone?" and in that moment any type of flirtation occurring with the cute actor and I was over. Because I immediately thought of my *perfect on paper* guy who happened to be out of town on a business trip. I began to tell my girlfriend my story and how I was planning to take it slow and not worry about insignificant things (like who he's following on social media) and I was going to live the story out. Then, she gave me the best yet odd advice I've heard for early stages of dating: *"Delete his number after every conversation."* At first I reacted questioning the maturity of her advice, but she had just gotten engaged so

I listened. She told me that when she first started dating her now fiancé, he didn't want a girlfriend although they were hanging out very frequently. She didn't want to get caught up or text him during moments of weakness aka drunk. So in turn she began to delete his number after every conversation. She realized that he was making the effort because it was always him contacting her first. In other words, he had to chase her. Men are hunters and they want to hunt us, but I am a lover and I want to love them. Nonetheless, I tried out her advice with my *perfect on paper* guy and every time I deleted his number a text from him would pop up. What also started popping up were his little flaws. Now, would I ignore them or use all of my attained experience from past relationships to avoid him–*and heartbreak*–all together?

I can write you a poem

Of course I can write you a poem.
Actually, the words would write themselves.
For you make me feel things
I thought I would never live again.
But why write you a poem,
When I can write out our story?
Why write you in a book,
When I can carve you in my heart?
Do you hear it palpitate?
Do you notice how when I'm in your bed
I fight against my sleep?
Why sleep through minutes
when I'm next to you?
Same minutes I can spend learning you.
Learning the freckles on your back,
And how you choose to love me.
Yes, I can write you a poem.
But truthfully why only write you one?
When I have a wellspring
of verses already dedicated to you.
Metaphors and analogies
helplessly clinging to my breath.
When you kiss me,
your passion consumes me
and eats me whole.
It might be pleasure
But why am I wishing
it defies time and words?

Is It a Crime to Want *More?*

My suitcase was packed and I was ready to go to Paris. For some people Paris is a dream world that screams romance and love. For me it screams hope. I know *hope* has been implemented in our minds as an American ideology, but for me there is nothing more hopeful than walking the streets of a beautiful city and watching strangers *French kiss*; at cafes, on sidewalks, on river steps, and pretty much anywhere! That's how life should be, we should express our love, and it shouldn't matter where we happen to be. It's ironic because I have been scared of PDA most of my life except for the occasional inebriated moment with someone I was extremely attracted to. Which takes me back to my *Perfect on Paper* guy. One night a girlfriend of mine saw us together and her face said it all. She was shocked! She couldn't believe that I was all over a guy in public. Well, let's make it very clear–*he started*. He was all over me and I loved it.

My favorite city awaited me which for me meant the joy of drinking champagne and eating croissants from my favorite boulangerie. Nonetheless, I wanted to stay on his mind while I was gone. I came up with the little idea of sending him a different French word or phrase every day during my stay in France. I had recently discovered an Instagram account that I absolutely adored because of its romantic posts of French words with a chic font. I took screenshots of some of my favorite words (obviously cropping where I got them from) and starting with the day I boarded my flight I began to send them to him. The purpose was to tease him with my choice of words, without scaring him. We weren't in that place yet for me to send him risqué pictures but a little mental stimulation never hurt anybody.

I slept very little during my trip and as Saturday night quickly approached a group of friends and I ended the night at a bar called Raspoutine. My phone was nearly dead and I was in desperate need to charge it. I headed towards the bar with the hope that the bartender would help me. To my surprise the bartender was *very* sexy. He eventually went out of his way to find a charger for my phone. Once my phone was charged I began to search for my daily *sexy* French word to send to my *Perfect on Paper* guy. In my head I began to think of options, but with every thought I also took a sip of my champagne and exchanged glances with the bartender. He was *very* attractive. I started taking trips to the bar with the excuse I needed more champagne. Leave it up to me to travel thousands of miles and fall for the bartender. We exchanged numbers and every night after every event I attended, I randomly ended up at Raspoutine ready to flirt with the bartender. The time arrived for me to return back home to Los Angeles. The bartender kept sending me messages every day. Proving how intense foreign men can be, but also how when a man is interested in a woman, distance will not deter him. Every day he gave me details of his day, shared with me what he liked, his aspirations, asked me a hundred questions to get to know me. Cursed *what's app* because he would've loved to see me face to face. Meanwhile, I began to compare his intensity to the lack of intensity I was receiving from my *Perfect on Paper* guy, and realized all the excuses I had made for him. I understood he was very busy with many responsibilities, and although his successful career was attractive in my eyes, in the end I am the type of woman who requires more attention. It didn't matter how amazing he made me feel when I was in front of him, I understood I wanted and deserved to feel amazing at all times. I needed consistency, and perhaps he wasn't ready to offer me what I desired. It's not a crime to simply want more, and it's not a crime that a bartender who lived thousands of miles away made me see that point.

Dream Girl

The irony of women injecting
Sizes into their hips,
All while I'm trying to reduce
My stubborn thighs.
Working towards the perfect ass
and the perfect abs.
Squatting these pressures away
All because I want to be your dream girl.
I want to be the girl you wake up for
I want to be the girl that you live for.
Sometimes I think my soul ain't enough.
I'm human,
I fight with insecurities,
Just like any other girl.
But if you love me
Why would you feed into them?
Because this life is no life
When I'm in competition with myself.
Tell me you love me not for my physical
But because we are entwined.
Why not live a story that supersedes
Everything that others expect us to be?
I know there are no guarantees
But let's make a pact.
This is you and I,
And all I want
Is to be your dream girl
Help me bring her out in me.

Will GREAT Sex *Imprison* You?

I have meditated a lot on *freedom*. In many countries, people revolt in order to gain certain freedoms, such as speech and religion. If you were raised in a Democratic culture you most likely tend to go about life thinking you already have *Freedom* because you don't live under an oppressing regime. But are you really *FREE*? Or are you a slave to certain things life has bestowed upon you? Like responsibilities with your family, career, and perhaps *even* love?

I began to think about certain times in my life in which I lacked freedom. I thought of certain relationships and separations. How when we argue with our significant other, we tend to *want to be FREE* from the relationship all together. Sometimes when you are going through *drama* in a relationship your girlfriends will always suggest it's time to move on. One evening during an after dinner Uber ride to the next venue where my girlfriends and I would continue our cocktails and frivolous girl talk on shoes; beauty regimens, and cutting off ex-boyfriends, suddenly my married girlfriend shouts out: "GREAT SEX WILL IMPRISON YOU!" In that moment all the noise disappeared and time stood still and I suddenly had a quick flashback of the times I had out of this world sex, and realized those were the boyfriends responsible for making me go crazy at one point or another. Now you may be wondering what made it *out of this world sex* and why on earth would I *FREE* myself from it? Experiencing great sex is truly a gift and a curse for both genders. A gift when you experience it and a curse to know what it's like to have it and then not have it anymore.

A good percentage of women are in love and having sex with a man they might adore but perhaps have never had an orgasm with. *Sadly, there are millions of women who wouldn't know how to stimulate and find their clitoris if their own life depended on it.* So many women making love and bringing life into this world yet have never experienced the pleasure of reaching climax. Then one glorious day if she's lucky she does and sometimes with who she least expects and that feeling of ecstasy will make her leave behind any ideology she had of "The Perfect Guy" because she'll find herself chasing the sensation of her *volcano erupting* again and again. She will chase that high until she realizes she's imprisoned by her new found drug. Because there are many men who are oblivious of how to make a woman reach an orgasm, it is quite possible a woman can find it hard to "FREE" herself from the man who did it well. The man who made her see stars when she closed her eyes while making love or *lust*. The same man who walks around with a huge ego, because although he can't afford all the things she likes–*No trips to the South of France with this guy*–he can always text her those awful words: *HE CAN'T FUCK YOU LIKE I CAN*. And that my friend is: **IMPRISONMENT**.

I looked at my married girlfriend and I asked her *"Have you ever been imprisoned?"*. She replied *"Aside from that one night I spent in Jail for a suspended license–**Yes I have**. My first boyfriend who I was with for five years and thank God I left him. I would've still been back home in my little town, with God knows how many kids, probably chasing his cheating-ass around town."* That depressing imagery of my beautiful and chic girlfriend being everything opposite of what she was today made me somewhat grateful to presently be "FREE" from the type of really good sex that imprisons you. Now I don't know for how long my freedom will last, but I can only hope that if I ever find myself imprisoned again, it would happen to be with an AMAZING man. You know, the type that can do all the things I like–*including orgasms and trips to the South of France.*

Prideful Hearts

My heart,
It still beats
when you look at me.
My skin,
It still feels your touch
off a look alone.
Maybe that's the nature of our souls
Familiarity even after lost years.
Our desire still shouts out
through skin pores
And through the walls
of our prideful hearts.

I Still Get Jealous

I might
Not
Be in love with you
Anymore
But why is it that I
Still
Get
Jealous,
When I
See
you
with her.

Letters, To Women Like Me

Do You Want to *Turn Back Time* or Do You Want *the Best*?

The main side effect of being single in a major city is experiencing a certain type of loneliness that I like to call *"shameful loneliness"*. Because how can I feel lonely in a city full of people and things to do? So what do I find myself doing frequently? I fill my social calendar as much as possible. I avoid clubs, but I will accept dinner invitations quite too often, meaning I've gained a few pounds but I am happier than sitting alone at home wondering why my last attempt at a relationship didn't work out or why did my *Perfect on paper* guy turn out to have a thing for bimbos.

It was a beautiful Friday in Los Angeles and one of my invitations for that day was a beauty festival put on by a big department store to celebrate the launch of a new makeup line by a world famous makeup artist. I attended the event with one of my best friends who loves the world of beauty. After a nice Q&A with the woman of the hour we began to walk around the festival and explore the different beauty tents. A few with the word **TRANSFORMATION** stood out. Immediately, a redheaded woman with a distinct British accent stopped me and asked me: *"Do you want your lips read?"* I had never heard of such thing but I was indeed curious. Right before I agreed I looked up at the sky and told

God that a lip reading couldn't possibly count as me seeing a fortune-teller, because how can anyone actually read lips? Oh boy, was I wrong! This woman said quite a lot, which left my friend surprised and I went on a search to see who else was doing facial readings. Eventually I came across the woman reading eyes. I sat down and wondered if she'd tell me anything in regards to my *shameful loneliness.* At first she told me about my creativity and goes on to say things that really didn't impress me much, until she mentioned my love life. She said I had to open my heart chakras. I was baffled considering I write, practice, talk about love on a daily basis. I got up, said thanks and if I had paid for her services I probably would've asked for my money back. How dare this stranger tell *me* of all people that I needed to open my heart chakras! Secretly, I went home and began to Google the subject and discuss it with friends.

One of my girlfriends who currently was in a very happy relationship after a string of men who were completely unhealthy for her, gave me her opinion. She told me that it's not only talking about the love we want but we must also practice it in every sense of the word. I proudly told her that I had closed doors with my exes and *any man* who was blocking the entry way for the next love of my life to enter. She said it was beyond that and suggested even a change in the books I read and the songs I heard. I understood that

❧

adjustment would create a shift in my love energy. In the end, what we surround ourselves with is what we attract. What we listen to, we believe. I understood that practice would be the key to open my heart chakras.

A few nights after that conversation, and as I got dressed for another event and listened to some music, one of my favorite Cher songs *"Turn back time"* came on. Like a child I danced around my apartment singing along the lyrics to the contagious beat. Suddenly, I stopped and asked myself: *Is this really what you want? Do you really want to turn back time and fix a broken relationship?* No, I wanted something better! I wanted *SIMPLY THE BEST.* I said goodbye to Cher and switched to Tina Turner and kept on dancing around my apartment feeling I *already* had the best! Singing badly but envisioning me telling the next man in my life *"You're simply the best, better than all the rest, better than anyone, anyone I ever met."* Perhaps the lip-reader wasn't wrong after all, maybe I did have to open my heart chakras, and maybe beauty festivals aren't meant to just *"Transform"* you on the outside, but also to shine a little light on how you're feeling inside.

Fragments

Little by little
when the hours
become days
and the days
become months
You will eventually
become fragments
of my memory.
Fragments of a love
Buried deep
in the shadows
of my past.

Does *TRUE LOVE* exist or is it just a FAIRYTALE?

Every year when Halloween comes around I procrastinate until the very last minute to put my costume together. Miraculously one particular year I knew I wanted to dress up as *Maleficent*. When I watched the film in the theater I burst out in tears because I related to the character so much. I genuinely felt that during a time in my life I had my wings clipped, and like Maleficent I was able to get my wings back. I sobbed because I recognized the pain she experienced. I knew how that resentment felt. There was a time I had carried a similar anger for someone I loved and I also knew how living with that shame felt inside.

Days leading up to Halloween with the story of Maleficent very vivid in my mind, I began to think on *TRUE LOVE*. What it is and how will we know when it's true? In other words, if I were *Sleeping Beauty*, who would have the power to break the spell with true love's kiss? One evening after having drank too much rosé I agreed to go to dinner with my ex-boyfriend. We were in a place in our relationship in which we were no longer trying to fix our broken past. He thought I told him what to do too much and I think I'm always right. Nonetheless, there I was in the car with him on our way to a restaurant of his choice. Not once did I feel I was digressing. After all, it was only dinner. While we were at the restaurant we talked about random things such as the food, the ambiance, his business, my next project, and then the conversation turned a bit serious and I gave him some advice. Then I said the words that either provide comfort or torture to his soul: "*I know you well. Remember, I know you better than anyone else.*" He smiled because he couldn't argue that. There was our life together and our life apart, but I knew every side of him. Even the sides he tried to hide from his family and certain people. Shakespeare wrote the lovely lines "*Love is blind and lovers cannot see the pretty follies that themselves commit.*" I had referred to love being blind since I was a teenager, but having him in front of me I understood true love was far from blind. You see the reason why I knew him so well was because I saw everything in him. I saw all of his flaws and all of his greatness. I accepted him for who he truly was and he knew that. That man seated in front of me also knew me well. He knew me so well that he also understood our bond. He understood our comfort. We left the restaurant and we both were very serene. Some would say it was the wine, but I knew it was beyond any alcohol. I felt peace knowing where we stood in each other's lives. Knowing that it didn't matter who we would go on to date, our love was true. I also realized that the idea of true love has been turned into a fantasy. People go through life thinking and wondering when they will meet their one true love. When in reality, one can have more than one true love and it doesn't always have to come in the form of prince charming. Sometimes to find a true love, means one must first stop being blind and see people for who they are.

Resentment and anger made Maleficent blind and all she saw was vengeance for having lost her wings, but Princess Aurora helped her gain her sight back. Maleficent for years watched over Princess Aurora to the point where she saw all of her sides and grew to love her. It was the true love Maleficent grew to have for Aurora that broke the spell. Maybe our idealism in love has made us desire a fairytale. We want the prince charming, the knight in shining armor, the happily ever after, but the truth is, falling in infatuation is the fairytale part. TRUE LOVE *is everything* after.

We weren't the same anymore

When he kissed me goodbye
something inside of me confirmed
that it was the end— for good.
That maybe I wasn't in love
with him anymore
but in love with the memories
of what we used to be.
Perhaps, that was the reason
he was able to reel me back in—
Our memories were strong.
They were irreplaceable,
but we of that time
weren't the same anymore.

I Am Human

I told him
I couldn't play his game anymore.
That he hurt me,
and I am human.
That's the thing about being human.
We feel.
We release tears.
Even when we fight
to keep them locked inside.

Letters, To Women Like Me

How *Much* Do *We* Lie to Ourselves?

Most of the time many of us fail to acknowledge the effect we have on the people around us. Sometimes out of pride and sometimes because of fear. When we remain quiet who are we hurting more? The people we love or ourselves? When I was younger I believed that opening up and divulging my feelings was a sign of weakness, or so I was told to believe. As I have grown into my own I have understood, that it's the contrary. It takes a brave person to admit how they feel. It takes an even bigger person to acknowledge and apologize. Some people believe admitting mistakes has a negative connotation as if one would be losing, but I choose to believe one only "loses" when one bottles things in. There is no freedom when you carry your secrets like a burden, because true freedom comes from honesty.

When I was a little girl my mother would tell my siblings and I that there was no sin bigger than the other, but if there is one sin that hurt God the most is when we lie. Now this always boggled my mind because what exactly did my mother mean by this? I eventually understood that God is love and lying is the complete opposite of love. It's deceit and death. Death because when you lie about someone you are assassinating that person's character and when you lie you are also assassinating your own character. You suddenly open the door to all types of things that are the opposite of love. Now this in no way means I have never lied. In many occasions I also have been weak. Within my weakness I have admitted my wrongs in order to set myself free. I believe one of the reasons a person cheats is because they have an inner desire for freedom. The irony is that when you cheat you end up with the opposite of freedom.

One night a girlfriend and I were catching up over dinner and somehow the men I wrote about in my first book 'Letters, To The Men I Have Loved' came up. Now believe it or not, I didn't write about many different men. The men I was involved with romantically were repeated in the letters. She brought up one of them specifically who turned out to be having an affair and it had become the talk in between certain circles. Mind you his wife had no clue and if she did, she was playing the part of a *beautiful fool* far too well. My friend went on to tell me that he confessed to her husband that he'd been having nightmares, and he knew he needed to straighten up. Now, apart from the story confirming to me that I had dodged a bullet, it also confirmed that lying takes you everywhere opposite of freedom. I began to think: *How much do we lie to ourselves? What must we learn to accept, so we can live in true peace and freedom?* I started to think of the different things I've done wrong, and possible solutions for me to change my patterns. Making mistakes is human but if it's a constant mistake, one must definitely give it attention. We are all souls having a physical human experience, not the opposite. Our experiences should help transform our souls to a better version. Lying to ourselves about situations, being the "beautiful fool" only keeps us stagnant. Lying to others to not hurt them, is like covering the wound with a Band-Aid. Divulging our feelings, confessing our truths whether to ourselves or whoever affected takes courage. A courageous task that will bring us an entire kingdom of peace and nightmare free nights.

There Were Days

Yes, it's true.
There were days I shut you out.
Yes, it's true.
There were days I ate my words
and spit them out.
Yes, it's true.
There were days my impulsivity
took the best of me.
Yet there were days,
I loved you more than others.
There were days,
I loved you beyond words,
gracefulness and cordiality.
Boundless moments
in which love reigned my heart,
And your breathing
controlled my heartbeat.
Moments that I'm willing
to give you over and over again.
It is in those same days,
In those same moments,
In which I understood infinity.
Because those were the days
I learned how it felt like
to love someone infinitely.

The Mirror and I

Sometimes I look at myself in the mirror
Not to look at my features
But to look at my heart.
I can't stare into a mirror
And lie to myself.
Lie about who I am
And what I feel.
Sometimes the deepest realizations
Occur during solitary moments
And a simple mirror.

Letters, To Women Like Me

WHY do *GREAT LOVE* stories end?

One Saturday afternoon as I organized my laundry I turned on my TV for some background noise. The trailer for the film *The Theory of Everything* caught my attention. The film is a biopic of the scientist Stephen Hawking who revolutionized science even while fighting a terrible disease. What I found interesting is that the trailer sold the movie as a love story. He often acknowledged his first wife as the reason he didn't die when he was given two years to live. The love and naiveté they both shared inspired his desire to live and overcome the obstacles of such a terrible disease. What I found even more interesting was how after 26 years of marriage they divorced. Why did such a great love story fall apart? With that story in mind I started thinking of other grand love stories that eventually fell apart, and I asked myself: *Why is it that some of our greatest love stories stop being great and eventually end?*

For days my attention gravitated towards famous love stories which did not survive the test of time, but when they were together these couples were out of this world. The Richard Burton–Elizabeth Taylor saga has always been a favorite. She on numerous occasions referred to Burton as the love of her life, and although he professed his undying love for her as well, he passed away next to another woman, his wife at the time. Obviously, there are always multiple reasons why people part ways, and things occur behind closed doors that only the lovers involved know, but one commonality became clear: All great love stories reach a certain height, sometimes the highest point that two people can reach together, but like one of the laws of physics states: "What comes up must come down." None of us are safe from it. So it's either staying in a balanced middle course or reaching the top with the potential of falling one day.

I began to think of my greatest love story until now, and although I hope I get to live an even greater one in the future, some things became evident. In that past relationship we were very different, but that made it more passionate. We were both extreme in everything we did, but the way our minds worked together was special. Our ideas synced in a way that was beyond artistic. We listened to each other and when we put those ideas into action, it became the beginning of something great. When we parted ways I felt I had given him an important part of me, whether it was a sense of confidence to achieve something that seemed like a dream, the support, the ideas, and the love of course. He definitely walked away with a truth that I'll always be part of in his mind. Something that till this day keeps him lingering around, unable to fully walk away from the bond we formed. I walked away with something from him as well, I walked away with an experience that allowed me to create a work that I'm currently very proud of. Although, to him we might still have a limitless amount of possibilities, it is a fact that *we are not the same of that time.* We had reached our height and physics got to us. He could blame me and I could blame him, but the fact is that we fell. Maybe not all great love stories are meant to last forever. Maybe they became great because only great love stories possess the power to inspire change and fuel greatness. Great love becomes a muse, whether to create, or to propel the desire to keep on living like in Stephen Hawking's case. The beautiful thing is that whoever experiences a great love story is lucky to reach the highest heights with anyone. If any human being can affect us to the point something absolutely great derives from that love, then that is the type of story worth living.

Goodbyes are always difficult

Goodbyes are always difficult.
No one ever taught me
what to do when things end.
No one ever taught me
what to do with stubborn memories
that still affect me every other day.
Now I'm learning how to act
when I run into you.
Now I'm learning how to plant
dry kisses on your cheek,
and keeping my arms all to myself.
I'm learning about awkward conversations
that always start with empty questions
such as: Are you doing well?
I'm learning about the art of evading eye
contact,
because I fear that in your eyes
I always see my soul.
It all feels like I'm learning
the meaning of bittersweet once again.
No one ever taught me
the protocol after a love story ends.
Saying goodbye to you was difficult,
and no one prepared me
for how cold it feels
telling others that it's over
and now "We're just friends".

People Like Him

He said, people like him end up alone.
He said, people like him aren't meant to be loved.

I looked at him and thought to myself:

All the more reasons
I'll never let go.
All the more reasons
I'll love you more.

Letters, To Women Like Me

Do We treat LOVE as a *"SALE"* or a *"FULL PRICE"* item?

Americans turn into another species when Black Friday rolls around. People will camp out for deals with the hope that they will save lots of money on their purchases. What I find interesting is that half the time people are purchasing things for the sake of purchasing, because our minds have been programmed to think *"You must get this now because it's on SALE!"*. I began to think of the correlation between love and the "Black Friday Sales" shopping tradition. How many times do we go on dates with people we wouldn't normally give the time of day simply because we've run out of options? Should we treat love as a "Sale" or wait for the love we yearn for at "Full Price"?

One evening I attended a basketball game with a girlfriend of mine and although I'm not very into basketball, I didn't want to pass up on the experience of sitting courtside at a Lakers game. My girlfriend and I made a date out of it and as we were sitting on the wood she spots a really cute guy. I told her to smile at him because a beautiful girl can intimidate a man, but the smile always gives the green light for him to approach her. Without realizing it another player had his eyes on her and her beautiful smile. After the game, he sent a runner to ask for her number. As a feminist I found that douchebag move completely egotistical. When the runner told her that Number X wanted her number she looked at me and whispered, *"Ugh, Number X wants my number"*. I looked at her and said to her, *"well you don't like him and if you give him your number you might ruin your chances with the one you do want"*. I expressed to her that when you really want a pair of shoes you will buy them at full price. If they are sold out, you will go the distance and even order them from another store in another state. You wouldn't settle for the shoes on sale simply because they are on sale. Her giving her number to *Number X* would've been like purchasing a pair of shoes on black Friday simply because they were on sale.

On my way back home I began to think what if we women began to treat everything in our lives as full priced items? We would work harder towards our dreams so we could afford all the full priced items! We wouldn't put up with shitty circumstances like waiting in line and shopping through racks, or fighting for a sale item. If we design our entire lives to only want and act as the full price items, that mentality has the power to change our entire lives. Not only how we look on the outside but most importantly how we feel about ourselves. We should set our sight on what we want and with confidence go after it. Many shoe designers say that if you give a woman the right pair of shoes, she will feel as if she can conquer the world. Now imagine if it were the shoes you truly want? Shoes you will cherish more than all the other shoes, and even when you've worn them many times you will still have a special place in your heart for them because they were so hard to get.

As I drove home I thought not only about shoes, but on how to apply that realization into my love life. I concluded that I want the *full price* man. I don't want my man *deducted* numerous times. I want him all in one piece, not broken, with scratches and with issues. Although, that immediately crossed out several options, it felt good knowing that I know what I want and that when I get him I'm going to cherish him more than all the rest, because he wasn't easy to find.

All at Once

So this is what it feels like
To be given
The sun,
The moon,
And the stars
All at once.

Is Age *Really* NOTHING but a Number?

When I was 6 years old my Dad would call me "Viejita" which in Spanish means "Little old lady." Turns out I had a habit of being a worrywart and always checked on things twice. Before I went to bed I'd check all the house doors and made sure no door remained unlocked. We lived in a safe neighborhood, but nonetheless I needed to make sure my family was safe. I turned off all the lights, because I believed in conserving electricity. My parents always treated me as if I was older because that's how I felt. What I can say is that anxiety had always been a part of my life, until I turned the age of thirty.

One weekend my ex's little sister who I've always considered the little sister I never had, came to LA with some girlfriends to celebrate her 23rd birthday. The Big 23! Because at 23 everything seems bigger than what it is. Everything seems more special too. Usually at the age of 23 you're discovering the world. She expressed to me how *old* she felt. I understood her post-college fears and expectations. She was racing with life instead of living it. On their second night in LA we went for pre-drinks before the club. Although, I am very much over going to clubs, when you're hosting a group of 23 year olds, a night-club always seems like a good option. At the restaurant the girls all shared with me a little bit of the happenings of their love life. I advised them that their early twenties should be their selfish years and they should focus on themselves. They should travel, explore and experience what life has to offer. I also told them that realistically when you live in a major city there is big chance that the boy you are dating at 23 won't be the man you end up spending the rest of your life with. They looked at me as if I said something sad. I told them to continue dating, because that was part of *living* but my advice was not to make a boy their entire world at such young age, but to instead focus their energy on their aspirations, and to trust that along their life journey they will eventually meet a man who will complement all their hard work. Afterwards, one of them told us her boyfriend had already texted her 24 times by the time we arrived at the restaurant. I turned to her and said *"his lack of trust is probably rooting from a place of unhappiness with himself and he probably feels insecure you might meet someone new who is doing better and leave him"*, she agreed and also expressed how she's over it. *At 23 I would be too.* They all told me they couldn't believe I was 30 because I looked and acted younger. I told them that I was very proud of the age of 30 because it became a very fulfilling time in my life. I felt very secure because I was happy with the woman I was becoming.

In your late twenties you dread turning 30 as if it were the end of your life. What I've understood is that at 30 my **REAL** life had just begun. My twenties were full of great memories because it holds many firsts. Yet, when you turn 30 you begin to realize that the things you felt were *big* at 23, aren't that *big* at all. The things I stressed about and allowed to drain my energy made me feel older then. When I became older I also became wiser at who and what I gave my energy to and that made my life more stress-free. Making me feel lighter and more youthful. I learned to say no and to choose my own path. I guess my father was wrong, when I was a child I didn't act like an old lady, I simply acted like a child with fear. Today, I go to bed and sometimes forget to switch off all the lights. Not because of carelessness but because at 30 I learned what I didn't as a child. I learned to take steps toward living a life without fear, and trust me that's a good life to live.

Imperfections

The thing
about imperfections
is that you never know
you have them
until someone decides
to point them out.

Why Is It That *Sometimes* It Is So Hard to *Let Go*?

It was time for me to move out of my old apartment and into a new apartment in Los Angeles. While I packed my belongings, I came across different objects from the past. It was interesting to compare who I was a few years ago with the woman I'm becoming. When I was about to turn off the lights in my old room, I took one last look at the view and said goodbye to all the city lights that flickered from afar. There is something sad about goodbyes. I felt I was saying goodbye to all the memories I built with certain people. I had been madly in love within those walls. I had also been the saddest. I even felt I was saying goodbye to the memories and habits I built with myself. There was a certain relief yet an equal amount of sadness. Why is it that sometimes it's *so* hard to let go? I found it easy to get rid of material things, but it was difficult to walk away from the memories built within those walls.

As I entered into my new home, I immediately felt peace about my new beginning. A new beginning, *literally*. I had even left my old bed behind, and was moving in with only a new bed, my clothes, books and art. When the movers left, I walked out to my balcony and took a moment to observe my new view. I noticed that now I had a view of the moon. In my old apartment I had an amazing view of the sun. As I observed the crescent moon I began to understand that life and its phases are like the sun and the moon, on opposite sides. For years I've compared men, women, and love with my fascination of our known universe. Life in general is like the sun and the moon. There are some phases in which we have so much fire within us. Either a fire that might build or a fire that might destroy. There are pink sunsets and sometimes the sky is full of clouds blocking the glory of the sun. At night it is the same with the moon. There are nights of full, crescent, or quarter moons. The only thing that changes is the view from where we can see it. When I left my old apartment I felt it was the death of a period in my life, but when I looked at the moon I understood that I didn't have to say goodbye to those memories or who I was years ago, I was only choosing to tuck them behind me, just like the sunsets were now tucked behind me. I will feel the sunsets and the sunrises, but now it was time to see the moon every night and allow a new phase to do its work in my life.

Sometimes we are so eager to start new that we think letting go of the past is the only necessary option, but maybe our present needs reminders of our past, just how our future needs our present. Perhaps, our past is not meant to be left behind entirely, but maybe it's supposed to exist like the sun in my case, tucked behind but still shining its light on my life. Change is necessary for survival, but the way we view those changes will depict the quality of our lives.

All My Parts I Left in You

Many times
I want to wish you
a lifetime of happiness.
But then my blood rises,
And certain images
cross my mind.
Of someone else
touching you,
Of someone else
having you.
I never thought
I'd be the jealous type,
But apparently
I'm possessive
Of all my parts,
I left in you.

In love with the Moon

I think I am in love with the moon.
Perhaps because it reminds me of you.
You are as unpredictable as her.
You are my forever natural satellite.
I can't escape you,
as you control my tides.
You orbit my life.
and illuminate my night.
I must say I am definitely,
in love with the moon.
Perhaps in the same way,
I am completely enamored by you.

Patching

We're done and I'm left
patching up my heart
like a warrior
patching up old wounds.
I don't show it,
but my God,
it still hurts.

How *Does* One Become *UNFORGETTABLE?*

Los Angeles is a city in which many of its residents currently work in the entertainment industry. Many people move to Hollywood to become a star, and for that same reason a billboard on Vine Street in Hollywood captured my attention. It was a billboard with the phrase "You don't have to be famous to be unforgettable." The purpose of the billboard was to promote *teach.org* with the end goal that it would improve the California teacher shortage. Not only did I think it was a genius-marketing tool, but I also found it to be very on point. I grew up with a mother whose profession has been teaching most of her life. I've held teachers on a pedestal because I understand the importance they are in our lives. A great teacher can inspire many and can change the world, but how does one convince a new generation that you don't have to be famous to be unforgettable?

In a world that is currently driven by unrealistic advertisements and social media platforms that do most of the influencing these days, how can we get back to the importance of quality and longevity? I began to think of my own life. How I also have wanted to impact people and be *unforgettable* perhaps since I first understood the word, and maybe since the first time I heard Nat King Cole's song *Unforgettable.* Because who doesn't want to be unforgettable? No one grows up and says they want to be unmemorable. Whether in our friendships, romances, career choices, no one wants to be forgotten and there is nothing wrong with that.

My mother teaches English Literature for Spanish speakers to 9th grade students in a predominantly Cuban area in Miami. She shared with me a specific story of one of her young female students. This teenage girl had arrived from Cuba not too long before and according to my mother she was an excellent student who strived to learn the language and aimed to succeed in the U.S after experiencing a difficult early life in Cuba. Earlier in the semester my mother shared with her students her favorite poem of mine titled *There, I Still Will Be*. She said that from that moment on that young girl read my work anywhere she could find it online, and wanted to name her future daughter after me. She had even asked her impoverished mother that the only present she wanted for Christmas that year was my book *Letters, To The Men I Have Loved*. When my mother shared that story with me I obviously began to cry like a little bitch. Of course it was sad that they were so poor that they couldn't afford my book, but I also cried because I understood how it feels to be inspired by a complete stranger. At her age I was also inspired by women who were not famous, or weren't considered the social ideal of how a woman is *supposed* to look or *be*. Often they were teachers, congresswomen, writers, and activists. They all left an unforgettable impact on my life. Of course we don't all choose the same paths and have the same outcomes, but we all have a choice to become unforgettable with our actions. Every day we are given the choice to be an influence whether in a positive or negative way. Every day we are given the choice to speak greatness into someone's life. Every day we are given the choice to smile, hug, and be thoughtful towards others. Every day we make the choice of making other people better or worse, and those choices are what eventually can make us unforgettable. Yes, we can make the choice to look presentable and have great taste, which will motivate others to look presentable as well, but our actions and words are truly the imprint we leave behind once everything material and physical has faded. Now, ask yourself what will you do today that will make you *unforgettable* to someone? Never leave behind what you can start today. Choose how you can impact others and recognize that what comes from the heart has no price and is the greatest gift of all.

Not the type

She's not the type who thinks
things are impossible.
She's not the type you love for a night,
and forget her existence.
Her voice will float beside your ear,
on your lonely nights,
like Shakespearean verses
that have survived hundreds of years.

Do you want a RESOLUTION or Do you want a SOLUTION?

A new year was around the corner and I began to think of resolutions and why is it so hard for people to keep them? Whether it's a resolution involving weight loss, employment, accomplishing a life-long goal, or moving on from a toxic relationship, it seems that most people fail rather than win. Or should I say most people Quit rather than Prevail?

I believe to fully understand the action behind a word, one must first understand its meaning. For example: Why is the word resolution used for every start of a NEW YEAR? If we break down the word from its prefix, we get RE and SOLUTION. "RE" is a prefix that means "AGAIN and AGAIN". For example: I REWRITE, I REPAINT, I REDO, I REMARRY, etc. I believe human beings in general have an idealistic point of view on life, especially in the beginning of a new year. We start the year full of expectations with the belief that we were given another chance at fulfilling our heart's desires. Perhaps that is the reason we believe in "RESOLUTIONS" because most of these "RESOLUTIONS" are what we didn't accomplish the previous year and we want to RETRY them AGAIN. I believe in getting up after any failure, but I decided I no longer wish for any *RESOLUTIONS*. What I desire in the NEW YEAR are SOLUTIONS!

I have a relative that all she does is blame God and others for any negative in her life. She says that she tries and tries but she can't catch a break. That when she applies for a better job, she can't ever get one. That when she prays for her baby daddy to change, he never does. Year after year I watch this woman remain stagnant. She gains more weight instead of losing, and sadly her lack of self-confidence is continuously present. Over Christmas Eve dinner I heard her tell another relative that she was "done" with her baby daddy, and she was going to kick him out. I turned to her and told her: *"You have been dealing with this man for thirteen years and you take him back over and over again. As soon as you take him back, you want to kick him out, because he never changes. All you've done is hurt yourself and your son. In regards to your lack of a good job, that has been your decision as well. You are talented and have a cosmetology license. You have a Bachelor's degree as well. You have options to apply for a new job but you have decided to drown yourself in self-pity."* To my surprise, she looked at me and said I was right. I love this woman and it saddened me that her SOLUTIONS were right in front of her, but she opted in wanting RESOLUTIONS to the same old problems.

Entering a New Year is a gift of another year of life. Why would you attempt to start the year with whatever you couldn't fix in the previous years? Things shouldn't be forced, because if something isn't working then maybe you need to do it differently. Life consists on making decisions. Our decisions mark our lives, our families, and our generation.

One day I made a personal decision that I wanted a solution for a sadness I was living with, and to accomplish life-long goals, so instead of me repeating the same cycle of everything that didn't work in the previous years, I chose to pay attention to the solutions in front of me. I chose to let go of everything that was blocking the solution, and to establish **the discipline** of working alongside the solution. Now do you want to fall into the idealism of *resolutions* or be brave enough to look at the problem and apply the **solution**? Deep inside we know the solution. We know we need to eat differently to lose weight, we know we have to graduate to have a career that demands a degree, we know that toxic relationships don't make us better but instead makes us feel worse. So I encourage you to **not** conform to your present circumstances, be courageous enough to seek the solutions, work towards them and be who you **are destined to be**.

The purge

It's Midnight
Pacific time
~~I lie still~~
Fetus position
As I purge you
out of my system.
On a cold bed
I'm sweating you out
like a fever.
Breathing heavily,
Inhaling boundless air,
While gasping for more.
I realize how much it hurts,
To carry such agony.
It hurts
To have the knowledge of this pain.
Heartbreak is a
dangerous state
And it can happen
at midnight
pacific time
or at any time of day.

Accept Your Heartbreak

Accept your heartbreak.
One cannot stop pain,
since pain is an emotion meant to be felt.
Cry if you must.
Let it consume you if you must,
and then allow it to be over.
Say goodbye after having fully experienced it.
Learn from it and learn the meaning of
decisions. Afterwards,
you will admire your courage and your strength.
Then you'll never allow anyone to break you in the same
way again.

Regrets Are Mostly Temporary

Regrets are mostly temporary.
There comes a day in which it all makes sense.
Every job you had.
Every class you took.
Every person you deeply connected with.
Every failure experienced.
Every lesson you learned as a child and as an adult.
The wisdom passed on to you by your elders.
The passions you had as a child
and all the new passions you garnered as an adult
with the maturity of time.
Every factor that makes you unique.
It all eventually makes sense
and if you're fearless
you'll use all that attained knowledge
and create the life you want to live.

Are our Choices *Aligned* with our Personal Vision?

One evening I received a phone call from a friend who I've known for many years and have witnessed many of her highs and lows. She started off the year in a very difficult state because she had lost her father on Christmas day. I genuinely believe there is nothing that can be said that can truly calm the heart of someone experiencing the unexpected loss of a loved one. All that can be done is to give love, support, and *to listen.*

She had just returned from her native country where the funeral services took place and during our conversation she mentioned she had a new boyfriend. I was somewhat perplexed because just a little over a month before we were planning a girls trip and there was no mention of a new boyfriend. Nonetheless, I was excited to hear all the details about her new man. She started off by telling me she had met him in 2009 and that he was forty years old. I know that forty might sound a little old for some women but when you're a woman who's in her early thirties you end up realizing most forty yr. old men act like they are still in their thirties, but usually they have a much better job than the average 30 yr. old man. She went into detail on how they reconnected and their first dates. They talked for hours, had great chemistry, he was attentive and then she told me what sounded like music to my ears: *He gave her and her family an unimaginable amount of support with the unexpected death of her father.* Instead of spending his holiday with his family, he traveled to the small town she's from in the Dominican Republic and basically watched her cry for days. He ate greasy food with the locals, bonded with her family and told her seeing her *un-glamourized* and connected to her roots made him fall in love with her.

When they returned to NYC he told her he was moving into a new apartment (*her dream apartment*) and he asked her to move in with him. I asked her: *"What are your goals in this phase of your life?"* She replied: *"I want to get married and have kids"*. I told her that we also needed to have a vision for our personal life with the same passion we plan our career life. Obviously, things never turn out exactly how we plan them. But I told her that if her goal was to get married and start a family; she should consider dating a different type of man than the men she's dated most of her life. She needed to be open to men who were ready to get married and start a family.

Relationships are all about timing and the only way to know if a man is ready is if he tells you that starting a family is what he wants at the **present** moment. Many men want a wife and family *someday,* but **not today.** I also told her that in comparison to all the men she's dated in the past, this boyfriend seemed ready to have a wife; a step closer to what she said she wanted.

After I hung up with her I asked myself: *What are my personal life goals?* I told myself that I might not be ready like my friend to get married and have children yet, but I know that eventually that's something I want in a few years. Then I understood that in the same way I prepare myself for future career opportunities, I should also prepare myself for the **right** man, for when the time comes. Unfortunately, there isn't a manual on *how to live life*, and we don't know what tomorrow will bring, but one thing I do know: *All the knowledge garnered from past mistakes and the ache previously experienced are the gems that life gives us to prepare.* The same way we trust the female body to naturally prepare to give birth, with time we must also trust that the **right** men naturally begin to stand out from the rest.

Promised Land

All of his flaws
Became my own.
For I made nests
Out of his darkest corners.
I found water
In his driest well.
I planted kisses
In his barren soil.
My love grew tall,
Within the cracks
Of a damaged heart.
Our love endured,
Standing firm
Like sacred oak,
In promised land.

What happens when our PHOBIAS get the best of us?

I have a guy friend who says he dated the "wrong girl" and began to vent about how after he spent a lot of money on this "wrong girl", he felt used and taken for granted and as a result he impulsively broke up with her. Although, he said he felt relieved and content, he still felt a need to vent about all the reasons why she was not good for him. He confided in me a bit too much about their sexual life. Which I was okay with because I don't have a problem discussing S-E-X with friends. He burst out, "*She didn't like to give me head!*" and I jokingly replied, "WAIT! *And you still bought her CHANEL purses and paid her rent?!*" Apart from thinking he was an idiot, I began to think I must be doing something wrong–*VERY WRONG.* How is it possible that many men like many women cannot tell the difference between the type of person you invest in and who you don't?

For a year he invested time and money into this girl who according to him didn't make him feel "very loved." So if he didn't feel loved, why did he stay with her? One very good reason, and a reason many of us have been guilty of at one point or another: **He didn't want to be alone.** Then it hit me, the feeling of loneliness is a common fear in humans and to avoid that feeling we sometimes open the door to people who are undeserving of us. I began to analyze my current love life and I realized I had been experiencing the opposite problem. Turns out I wasn't investing much time in any man. Apart from text conversations and dates here and there, I was too busy investing time in myself. In my case I didn't suffer from *EREMOPHOBIA* (fear of being with oneself or loneliness) like my friend. Turns out I had developed a different phobia. I developed *ATELOPHOBIA*, a fear of imperfection. Because what if what I think is great is great, but there is something *GREATER?* So I always found something wrong in the men I would go on dates with. My desire to fall madly in love with a quality man turned me into a busier sex-less social butterfly. I began to think of ways of how to get rid of my ATELOPHOBIA without compromising the traits I'm looking for in my next man.

At the time while seeking for a solution I received a text from an old friend who had been living in another state for some time. He was visiting LA for work and informed me he purchased *Letters, To The Men I Have Loved* and read it on his flight. I adored the gesture of support and met up with him to catch up. As we sat for tea I was reminded of how beautiful he was. His hair, his perfect skin and features and his hypnotizing smile had me floored. The amazing conversation we had made me want to pinch myself and at times I mumbled my words because I was NERVOUS! I looked him up and down, looking for an imperfection–*because he must have several* I thought. Nope, he could also dress well. Then he mentioned his age, a factor I completely had forgotten about–*he was younger than me!* Younger when I want older. One of my friends joined us towards the end of tea and after he said his goodbyes, she turned to me and said *"What's wrong with you?! Why haven't you made a move on that?!"* All the reasons of why I shouldn't date a man in his twenties emerged. Would I take a risk of pursuing an amazing man who is in his late twenties or let my *ATELOPHOBIA* get the best of me once again?

Cut Me Open

Cut me open!
Provoke emotion in me.
I am no longer broken,
But I'm worse,
I'm numb—can't feel a thing.
Cut me open!
Return the feelings you stole from me.

Should Age be *a Factor*?

I celebrated my birthday with a weekend long festivity. I organized champagne brunches and dinners with people I love. While being out I couldn't help but to think of my crush, our age difference and my traditional mindset of preferring older men. I thought to myself: *Should age be a factor when determining whether or not to proceed?*

My guy best friends who are all older than me advised me that men living in a major city usually aren't ready until thirty-five. Meaning that if he's under 35 he is probably still in *"Fun Mode"*. Now was I willing to risk the possibility of it being a "Fun Story" instead of a "Love Story"? Whatever the future held something was certain: I would give him the green light. But how was I going to do that? Believe it or not I'm somewhat shy when it comes to men, especially one who happens to be such an Adonis. My friend who met him while he was last in town suggested for me to start dropping hints of my interest in him during our conversations. So that day between brunch and dinner I was extra confident due to all the champagne in my system, and I sent him the super generic text *"Wish you were here"*. Mind you I was in bed trying to muster the energy to get ready for dinner. He asked where I was and my plans for the evening and I texted him back, *"I'm at home. Alone. In bed. Naked."* What better way than to give him a hint that I was interested. It doesn't matter how good a man can be, what values he holds dearly, a man is still a man and the word *"Naked"* will spark his imagination in a heartbeat. The conversation turned very *exciting* and a highlight of my weekend. Why? Because we all need a little thrill in our lives. During our conversation he mentioned the word *"Adventurous"* and how he lives by it. Then it hit me *"Adventurous"* is his ability to take risks which is the youth in him. So as we physically age do we stop being as adventurous? Do we start thinking more with our brains and less with our hearts? Do we take less risks in love, because aging brings along all the vivid memories of painful experiences from our past? After he shared some of his long list of adventurous escapades, I began to think of mine. I realized that I've had many adventurous moments in my early twenties, but I've lacked adventure in the love department in the past year. Had my desire to plan my future lead me to lack adventure?

We are taught to plan our future based on the idea that responsible people know what they want, but the best stories are like the best success stories: They involve risk and can't be planned. So after he shared with me his view on life, I asked him *"Am I a risk?"* and he replied *"Do you want to be?"* and just like that I made the choice I would have adventure in my 30's, just how I had it in my 20's. I will forget the notion that age is a factor. I will be open to experience, even if it has the possibility of ending in tragedy. **I WILL LIVE** each day because adventure is living the moment, and so many people age each year and celebrate countless birthdays without ever actually *living*.

I'm Curious

I'm curious about your laugh,
and why you always choose red wine.
I'm curious about the innocence,
that lies behind your eyes.
I'm curious to caress your face
and pull it very close to mine.
I'm curious to feel your lips,
on the erogenous weakness of my neck.
I'm curious about your heart,
and how many times
if any,
it has loved.

All or *Absolutely* NOTHING?

One phrase that I use to describe myself is *"All or Nothing"*. You can say that I'm a bit on the extreme side, but I can't help being any other way. When I'm in love I am ALL in. There are no blurry lines after I make a decision. During a group outing a new male friend said he was the same way. He had recently broken up with a girl after living a passionate affair that lasted only a few short months. So when he said he was "All or nothing" I was curious as to what she did that made him break up with her considering he was very into her but I didn't want to pry, because I was intrigued by him and the last thing I wanted was to become his therapist and discuss his ex.

This group outing turned out to be insanely fun and filled with too much liquor. We ended up at this super cool Cuban rum bar called *La Descarga* in which I hadn't visited in months. To visit you must make prior reservations and when you arrive a hostess walks you through a doorway that on the outside looks like a closet. The closet takes you to a spiral staircase and that night for a quick second I felt I was "*Baby*" from *Dirty Dancing*, without the watermelon of course. We walked into a dark room of people dancing to salsa music and the smell of cigars and rum were potent. I felt I was about to do something *really bad*. The type of bad things you only do in foreign countries because no one knows you. It was a group of seven and the liquor was pouring. A few familiar songs began to play and I *started dancing*. The inebriated Latina in me did what she knows best–*I gave a sensual performance* and my newly single friend watched. Suddenly I felt his hands on my waist turning me around to face him. He leaned over and began to kiss me. I didn't push him back, I pulled him closer. I taught *the gringo* a few steps and how to move to the rhythm of salsa. The night continued and it felt endless. Anyone observing us would have thought it was the beginning of a love affair or a *one-night affair*. But when it's two people with similar mindsets you can truly end up with all or absolutely nothing.

The next day I went about my day and I walked around as if I had a dirty little secret. I felt somewhat empowered on having done something out of my character. The fact that I also never replied to any of my ex's text messages while I dirty danced with my friend also felt empowering. That evening I randomly ran into *my new friend* at Soho House and I acted nonchalant because I genuinely have so much fun with him that I would never want to make it awkward between us. I sipped on rosé wine, as he told a few stories, because he's a great story teller. During one of his stories he mentioned his age. I looked at him in disbelief because he looked, dressed, and acted much younger. But what shocked me the most was that he was exactly 20 years older than the younger guy I was recently crushing on and they shared the same name. *Same name as my ex as well.* **The same ex I was trying to avoid.** I began to question what on earth was I doing that suddenly I kept attracting that name into my life–*over and over again.* Was it possible that it was my heart calling out parts of my ex? Or was it possible that I was looking for him in somebody new? That I was fighting so hard to cut him out of my life that all I was doing was attracting people that reminded me of him? So what to do about my heart after I made a pact with my brain? I'm "All or Nothing" therefore I understood there was a decision I had to make. As all these questions ran through my head *my friend* tempted me and whispered to me he wanted to be in my next book. I smiled and replied: "*No, you don't. No, you don't*".

Signs

There I stood
looking into another man's eyes,
listening to the pattern of his laugh.
When a certain rhythm caught my ear,
it was our song playing in the distance,
yet so clear.
I closed my eyes,
and asked myself: Was this a sign?
Proving you indeed still count,
when it comes to the haunting of my heart.

Like Magnets

How did we end up here?
Our bodies on one another
My head on your chest,
Your hands tangled with mine.
We must've met in a magnetic field,
A place where emotions attract,
And all logic repels each other.

Letters, To Women Like Me

Is It Possible to *Re-fall* in LOVE?

Throughout the process of writing my first book I relived many memories of the men I wrote about. One theme became clear *"Love can subside but it goes nowhere"*. However, love can change its form. But, after it subsides is it possible to revive it? Is it possible to re-fall in love?

Recently a very close friend of mine sent out a group text with the news she became engaged. I was nearly shocked when I saw the picture of the ring. Who proposed to her? I was so confused. She wasn't dating anyone. She was a single mother, but with a *baby daddy* that still loved her. He is a great father as well and after a two-year separation period she began to spend quality time with him because of their son. I encouraged it because I felt her son needed a constant father figure in his life not only every other weekend. During one of these "family" outings he expressed to her how he wanted to make it work with her and how much he still loved her. She expressed to him her reservations, but she was willing to give it a try again. He became very excited and within two weeks he proposed and she said YES! When she told me the engagement story I couldn't help but to ask her if she was 100% sure that's what she wanted. In the end, I believe in love and never settling so I wanted to make sure she was in love with him–*again*.

She told me that she felt no hesitation and for months she prayed for God to restore the passion and love she once had for him. *Apparently, God listened to her prayers.* Although, I believe in the power of prayer I wondered how was it possible to fall in love again with someone who you fell out of love with?

I came across some old writing of mine, and a line stood out: "*Love is the resurgence of memories everyday*". Staying in love has two factors: First is the history between two people, and the other is timing. If you spend enough quality time with someone you will form a bond. I believe it's truly possible to fall in love with someone off of quality time alone and that is a choice we make. Attraction is the factor that makes us want to spend quality time with someone. In my friend's case her decision of spending quality time with her ex allowed them to reconcile but what if you're single without an ex to reconcile with? Why not fall in love with yourself first before falling for someone new? Why not spend quality time alone, and get to know yourself better? Nourishing your core because certainly the relationship we have with ourselves determines the quality of our relationships with others. That day I made the decision to re-fall in love with myself as many more times possible. Not only because it's romantic but more because I deserve it.

I Want You

I want you.
no I don't.
      I lied.
I do want you.
maybe I want you
because I love you.
I can't stop loving you
      even
when all my heart wants
is to not want you.
and for someone new
to come in
      and
convince me differently.

What do our Dreams *Tell Us?*

It was a beautiful Friday in January and I traveled to Santa Barbara for the weekend to celebrate a friend's birthday. I hadn't seen some of the girls she invited in months, so apart from what can be seen on social media they didn't have much clue to the recent happenings of my personal life. I learned the hard way about posting relationship pics and cute "date" pics on social media. I now prefer to keep that part of my life private.

At dinner one of the girls asked me what was happening with my ex-boyfriend. It was common knowledge to people that knew us that we were friends again and even flirted with the idea of rekindling our love story. We went on dates, and sometimes slept together and my excuse for it was that I preferred to sexually recycle instead of adding on mileage with new men I hardly knew. But the game we were playing quickly became old. In the end, you remember why you broke up in the first place, and you realize it's the familiarity you both have that keeps you holding on to the past. I told the girls I had a moment of clarity through a dream I had not long before. In the dream I saw the three men I had been flirting with including my ex. It was very obvious that the dream was foretelling a decision I had to make. I had decided to amicably cut ties with my ex because he was holding me back from fully connecting with the new men that entered my life.

This was not the first time I've made a decision based on a dream. I've been studying the meaning of dreams since I was a teen. For me a dream is a doorway to the spiritual world, and it is a method our soul uses to speak to us. Dreams are never what they seem. It is symbolism for certain things in your present and future life. In one night a person can have hundreds of short dreams. We never remember all the dreams we have, but the ones we do remember are the dreams we are supposed to pay attention to. As the night continued the girls began to share some of their recent dreams. One of the girls dreamt she was urged to give attention to her masculine side, as she had been focused on her feminine side for the last five years. She is a devoted mother and when she decided to give 100% to her family she neglected her work. The dream motivated her to renew her passion for her career. I found it fascinating that I wasn't the only person who follows the path of their dreams.

When I returned Los Angeles I watched a film a friend recommended. The movie is titled "i Origins" and presented two different types of people; the Atheist and the Spiritual. The spiritual character tries to convince her atheist boyfriend that God exists. In the film her character considered the soul to be the connection humans have with the creator. Her character also believed that the soul continues living on after our physical death. I was in tears by the end of the film and I began to ask myself questions. I began to question my dreams and my essence. The things I've been drawn to since I was a child. Things that felt too familiar when I saw for the first time, or the men I fell in love with that I felt I knew from some time before. Because how do you really tell someone you feel you know them from another life without sounding crazy? How do you tell them that they fill a vacancy and it's possible that your souls brushed paths before? I also thought about the future and if it was possible to make a profound connection with a brand new soul?

When it comes to the origin of life and spiritual questions regarding the soul one will never find a concrete answer and any conviction perhaps relies on a "gut" feeling we all have, and our own individual truth. Certainly, decisions made using your "gut" will provide peace; the same kind of peace one can experience while driving along the seacoast. The view of a magnificent scenery and the fresh air will make you want to stay on the road, and not return to the chaos of a loud city. Although, we can't prove if dreams and souls are inter-connected, maybe they are meant to exist to provide us with that feeling of peace.

A feeling that's necessary in our human journey whether with love or in moments we need reminders in order to press on, and to stay driving on the road.

Unsaid

I'm guilty of holding on to the past,
because I was unsure
of what the future might bring.
If I could hold you
one last time,
I'd tell you all the things
I'd like you to remember me for.
But some things
are better left unsaid.
Because there aren't any right words to say
When we both know that it's over,
and we'd be crazy to try again.

Letters, To Women Like Me

Is Love JUST a Chemical Reaction?

"*Yes according to science love is a chemical reaction.*" that's what I told a group of friends over lunch on a cold afternoon in New York City. "*Humans, like animals were created to procreate, so in order to do that a certain attraction must occur. One in which involves hormones and smell. We are simply attracted to each other's natural smell. But then that eventually begins to subside and mature love occurs. Which is a bond based on friendship and mixed with common goals between two people.*" One of my girlfriends who recently became engaged agreed and added "*Yep, most of the time it's all over in the first two to three years.*" I looked around and started thinking of attraction and how it's even more unexplainable than love. When we're asked why we love someone we begin to come up with reasons. But when we're asked why are we attracted to someone sometimes we become speechless. Half the time, there's always an "*I don't know BUT...*"

After our lunch I kept thinking about our conversation. I've always been a firm believer that if you spend more than enough quality time with someone you can learn to love that person. They can eventually grow on you, but the smell factor intrigued me particularly after re-reading one of my poems "*The Angel*" from my book

Letters, To The Men I Have Loved. I begin the poem with the line *"His distinct natural smell, I loved to smell the soap off his bare chest"* and I remembered his natural smell, and of all the other significant men before him and I became curious. What if I'm simply "smelling" the wrong men? What if my deviated septum is to blame for my failed attempts at long-lasting love? Okay, Okay I kid! I shouldn't blame my deviated septum for my decisions but what if there is some scientific formula to "smell" a *correct* partner? With that thought in mind and me being sick as a dog (due to the insane weather change I had drastically experienced) I found myself fighting to breathe, and without the ability to smell anything properly. Although, I was sick, I couldn't stay in during my entire stay in NYC so I stepped out and *headed to The Mercer to for dinner.* From afar I saw a man sitting alone, he was dressed in black, and had five o'clock shadow; both weaknesses of mine. I was close enough to him that I was able to properly check him out. There was a certain mystery about him. After his check arrived, I lost him. He must've made his exit, but nonetheless he made an impression on me. What's interesting is that there was no way I could have smelled him from afar; my attraction to him was purely visual. Like when we are attracted to certain clothes or pieces of art. If his aesthetic would've been different I perhaps wouldn't have gravitated towards him. So I began to think that perhaps the formula in love is a combination of sight and smell. Then I told myself who am I kidding? I don't look at love as a science. Although science has tried to prove love exists by using theories of hormones and attraction; love itself is unexplainable and supernatural. We feel it but can't see it. I concluded that some people will bring out certain senses more potently than others, but the only formula for a long-lasting love is when all five senses are involved. The person who attracts all your senses gets all of you: *your sight, your smell, your hearing, your taste, and your touch.* Maybe, it is both science and a feeling at the same time, and maybe our senses hold the hidden clues in order to know when we've met *the one.*

Come Closer

Come closer to me,
I want your scent
Concentrated on my clothes.

Come closer to me,
I want you to be the last scent,
I smell once my eyes close.

Where Is *Your* Home?

Los Angeles in my opinion has to be one of the best cities in the world. It took me *years* to realize it. In fact, during my first years living in Los Angeles I always found something wrong with it because part of me always felt it would be temporary. I'd fulfill my destiny and then move on to another city and conquer other dreams. Today, I find myself in love with Los Angeles! I look at its sunsets and sunrises knowing that perhaps other cities possess better sunsets and beaches but my heart at this time feels content with this one. That's exactly how romantic love feels.

One night while being a couch potato and flipping through TV channels I came across the film *"When Harry Met Sally"*. This movie for some might be considered an antiquity but I still think it's perhaps one of the best Romantic Comedies ever made. I got cozy and prepared to watch the remaining hour of the film. As I analyzed certain parts of the movie and noticed how so many parts of the story would be completely different today due to technology; a young Meg Ryan captured my undivided attention. Her character, Sally, was crying hysterically to her friend Harry because she had just found out her ex was getting married to the rebound. Harry asked her *"Would you take him back?"* Sally replied *"NO"*. You see, Sally was no longer in love with her ex but her ego was hurt. She felt her ex for all those years didn't want to marry *HER, and that he felt she wasn't the one.* Unfortunately, like many men, women make the common mistake of not understanding the difference between a **hurt ego** and a **broken heart.** Still, part of me felt empathy for Sally and the feeling of unworthiness she was battling. It's tough to see someone you loved deeply happy with a woman that's not you. Another part of me was upset that the screenwriter just left her without a proper response from Harry. The reality is that Sally did nothing wrong in her relationship with her ex, she indeed was worthy to be loved correctly but both men and women are ready for marriage at different times. Commitment in love is all about timing. A lot also depends on the maturity of the two lovers involved. The moment we become ready, whoever is in our lives or whoever we meet next will most likely get the cake– *The Wedding Cake that is.*

During my early twenties I met great guys that deserved my love, but for whatever reason it wasn't my time to fully commit to any of them. Perhaps, I dated the complicated ones because it was exciting at the time and I saw myself reflected in them. Who knows? But I do know that there was one time I felt ready to commit. I wanted *the house with the white picket fence with my guy and I was devoted to him* and our relationship. Perhaps, if it hadn't been him it would've been someone else, because the reality was that it was me who was ready. Our story eventually ended and I was back in the dating pool. After, a number of people gave me advice on what to do, what to expect, who to date, but I've learned that *life just surprises you* and sometimes you won't see the best parts coming. You might not feel ready for what life brings you at first. You might find a hundred reasons why certain things are not for you, but then a moment can change everything. Suddenly everything will feel right even in the midst of chaos. You will feel peace that you are exactly where you need to be. Just like how one specific day years ago, I realized I missed LA. I missed the perfect weather, the sunsets, and its early nights. And when I returned I whispered to myself *I love you LA*. That day I genuinely felt it truly was my home, just like how that one specific time I felt ready to commit to someone who I felt was my home too.

Wherever I am

Wherever I go
You will be welcomed.
Wherever I rest
You will rest.
Whatever I know
You shall know.
Wherever I am
Is your home.

Your Skin is My Home

Your skin is my home
Warm
Smooth
Perfect, Tone.
Your skin is my home
Tender
Addictive
Immensely, Whole.

Letters, To Women Like Me

Do You Miss *Him* or The Feeling?

I had just lived one of those weekends in which I had exhausted my body with too much fun. When Sunday night rolled in all I wanted was to vegetate on my couch and watch one of my favorite shows. While I *made love* to my couch, ordered delicious Thai food, and drank *lots* of water. I received a text from the man who never lets me go, even after I've told him over and over again that I am over him and his ways. Nonetheless, I replied and just like that another conversation with my ex ensued *again*. I was so mellow that I was genuinely nice to him because I had no energy to argue or attempt to analyze his *flirty-full of desire* text messages. And that's what our relationship had become, a man I once loved so much was now a man who I had phone conversations without any hope or desire of rekindling our love story.

I eventually passed out on my couch with my phone on hand and I woke up around 3 am with a burst of energy. After I picked up my plate and leftovers I headed towards my room. I lied down and my bed felt so cold. I contemplated on adding another blanket as I put on fuzzy socks and curled up in fetus position when suddenly I missed having a boyfriend–*I actually missed him and being in our bed together, him holding me the entire night, how he used to hold me.* I looked around and noticed I was on the left side of the bed. Which was odd considering that for a long time I'd been sleeping in the middle. I was disappointed in myself as if I knew better. I realized I was experiencing a moment of weakness. A moment that tricks you into thinking that it doesn't matter what you accomplish in life, what you buy, where you travel, if you don't have someone to share it with, it won't be as great. Because like this old woman told me a long time ago, my career will not hug me at night. I hated feeling weak so I got up and turned on my heater because I refused to think that if I had someone next to me I'd feel any less lonely or any much happier. To make it worse the next day was a busy day of running errands with an unexciting visit to the dentist. I was so numb and in pain by the time I left, and the only positive thing was that I couldn't eat—*which is always a great thing when you want to lose a few pounds.* It was definitely the type of day you want for someone to *baby* you and spoon you with affection. I arrived back home and it was time to unload my car. I bought too many things for my home and had no one to carry them up. Then it hit me! I am *really* a single girl in the city of angels. Was it okay to be an independent strong woman, and yet still need MEN?

I realized we will still want men even during an age in which sometimes a vibrator does a better job at pleasing a woman than many sexually clueless men out there, but the question is: *Do we still NEED them?* Then I understood living alone is like natural selection, single people must adapt to doing everything on their own: self-sufficient living. Human beings are not meant to be alone but sometimes that's our reality, so until we find a partner who truly deserves us then we should have a stronger outlook on life and stronger arms, because the BBQ grill I had just bought and was super excited for won't be assembled on its own.

Soul Ties

When good things happen
you're the first person
I want to share it with.
Sometimes, actually many times I see things
and I think to myself:
He'd like that.
At times I start laughing hysterically
at something ridiculously stupid
and think to myself:
He'd be so annoyed right now.
I guess that's what happens
when two people become one
and then they part ways.
Their physical body is gone
but the essence of their soul mixed with yours,
and even if you try
it's extremely hard to undo.
Some people call it soul ties
but I call it my soul is missing you.

Can We *HAVE IT ALL?*

International Women's Day is a day that every woman should embrace. We should feel proud of being born women and pass on that pride to other women around us. I figured I'd share part of a speech I gave at Syracuse University. I hope it empowers and reminds you that as women we have been oppressed, objectified, treated as property since the beginning of time and as women we need to unite and be twice militant. It is our duty to make each other stronger and teach our future daughters the strength and courage that is needed to persevere and turn our dreams into reality.

*A certain confidence comes with knowing who you are! You know what you won't tolerate, you know what you like, you know who you want to be, you know what type of people you want to love and you know who deserves your love! A woman who **knows** what she wants will **fight** for what she wants, and she can become a powerful force in any arena. After releasing my first book "Letters, To The Men I Have Loved" to the public I learned that I wasn't alone. Sometimes when we experience pain and loss we feel that no one is able to understand our pain. But I learned that there were women like me. Women that at one point loved and* then lost but didn't dwell in the pain. Instead they accepted their pain, they accepted their heartbreak and they became determined to **overcome** it. The reality is that heartbreak is just another obstacle that blocks you from living the life you dream of living. Maybe, some of you have never experienced romantic heartbreak but I'm sure you've at some point experienced disillusionment and failures. These failures will eventually shape you and you will have the choice to decide what to do with it. Will it make you or will it break you?

During a work meeting with a woman who's not only a friend but someone I've admired for years, she asked me: "What is next for you? What do you want to do next?" I told her that I was enjoying my journey and I was living every moment. Focused on the next career goals on my list, enjoying being single, exploring and taking my time to meet the right men because eventually I do want a family. She told me that when she reached a certain age she wanted to get pregnant and she wasn't conceiving right away. Then when she was about to produce a huge blockbuster and very demanding film that needed all of her attention Bam! She got pregnant. She allowed for nature to take its course instead of feeding into the negative opinions of others. She looked at me and told me: **"WOMEN LIKE US CAN HAVE IT ALL, DON'T LET ANYONE TELL YOU DIFFERENTLY. WOMEN LIKE**

***US CAN HAVE THE POWERFUL CAREER AND HAVE
THE FAMILY TOO."*** *I looked at her and in that moment I
knew why I had looked up to her for so many years. She knew
who she was, and any setbacks never stopped her. I said to
myself:* **I am like her.**

*I'd like to tell you that you are no different than my
friend or I. Women like you and I can have it all. The only
determining factor is if you want it. Life is all about decisions.
When I've met fans of my books and they tell me I have
inspired them to do what I did, to turn the pain into greatness,
I am immediately moved. Not only because it's humbling
but because it's a domino effect. Me becoming stronger and
sharing part of my journey made another woman stronger.
That woman will pay it forward and it creates a movement. A
movement of women that not only know about love "beyond
ideologies and poetic words", but a movement of STRONG
WOMEN who know what they want, what they deserve, and
most importantly women who know that if they choose, they
can have it all too.*

My loving Gaia

Oh! My loving Gaia
How I miss our night walks,
Your ear always heard me speak
My dreams unto the moon.
I'd lock myself in my room,
When my tears I tried to hide.
Your subtle door knock
I always heard through.
"Treasure— estas bien?"[11]
I know your heart,
was breaking the same.
As twins feel each other's pain,
You must have passed me
more than just your name.
I'd like to think it was strength and grace.
But from everything that you possess,
What I admire most is your unwavering faith.
Most would say those are queen traits,
But your gifts live beyond
A throne and stage.
You bore my oceans of complexity,
You bore my thunder of bravery,
You bore my sea of love,
You are my earth in each calamity.
Oh! you are my forever loving Gaia.
My mother goddess,
The purest side beneath my soul.

1 "Are you ok?" in Spanish.

Just Like You

I keep a smile on,
Like a pageant queen.
Can't let the real world know,
Of what they are too blind to see.
So I dress up all my fears away,
Tasting salty tears along the way.
They call me beautiful and a lucky girl.
It's nice to know,
But can't they tell, I am more?
They think the pretty girl
doesn't experience pain,
Except when she gets raped,
Because she gets everything her way.
There's people dying
every second of the day,
And we will never know their names.
Some of them heroes in their own right,
Because struggle was all they knew
Their whole lives.
I can't say I've seen my brother die,
But I can say that if he does,
I'll shed the same tears you cried.
Although we might be from different tracks,
We share insecurities,
That only love can heal with time.
So why try to segregate our struggles

And blame each other for what we each don't have?
For in the end,
A common truth we do have.
We all live and will someday die.
So let's get along,
While there's a chance in sight.

Dear Woman,

She is not your enemy
nor does she have to be.
She is not your competition
because you are enough.
She has been oppressed,
just like you and your mother
and your mother's mother.
She has her own dreams,
just like you have your own.
She can be special
and so can you.
She can't stop your destiny
nor you can stop hers.
She loves and has been broken,
have you forgotten how that feels?
For it was a woman
who carried you in her womb.
It was a woman
who pushed through a generation
of painful curses
to bring you into the world,
why would you turn against her?
Why break her?
When you can uplift her.
Why fight her?
When you can unite
and find your power together.

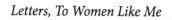

Letters, To Women Like Me

Should Love Have a SET of *Rules*?

One night I received a text from a girlfriend that said: *"I'm reading this book on dating rules, and I'm over here like I did it all wrong."* I replied impulsively *"Don't read that! It's not the same for everyone."* But was I wrong? *Do we need rules to date better?* For some reason I've felt that the only way to date better is to make mistakes and try to get it right the next time around. From my mistakes I've noticed that if we treat the guys we like as the guys we don't like, most of the time they'll act better because they feel they haven't conquered us. Sounds like too much work right? My friend began to share with me the parts of the book that resonated with her. There was a part on how men need the chase, and to feel *like men,* because at times some women emasculate them. I began to think the world is at a transition stage in regards to gender roles.

For centuries women played the same role of being pursued and of being submissive. They'd get married and half the time eventually cheated on with a mistress that played a completely different game. Fast-forward to today and women now find themselves at a crossroad of not knowing where our role stands. We can be career women with the ability to do anything a man can do, but we still want to feel like **women**, because the seed of what a woman *is supposed to be* was planted in us since our birth. Generations after generations a society programmed by ideologies always deriving from a man's perspective that has continuously instructed women on how they're supposed to look, act, and be. Countless books written to teach women how to be a proper wife, and a doting mother, but not enough books to motivate women to follow their hearts' desires. Perhaps, that is the reason why I replied *"Don't read that"*. **Should love have a set of rules?** Or should it be instincts based on real emotion? Have we ever thought that the heart can't be controlled and treated like a game? That the only way to live a life without regrets is to do it your way and not anyone else's? Shouldn't we trust the process and leave it up to timing? Shouldn't we be less anxious and live in the present? Or maybe, do we think too much? Do we try to look for answers in questions that aren't meant to have answers? We try to give life to relationships that are dead because we are human and we hope that things might change.

As I've grown older I've learned to just **BE** and to live even the questions. I can't beat myself over and over again for my mistakes or how I could have done things differently at one point in time, because what's done is done. Like my friend I can also read books on dating rules, and *how he's not into me* but in the end I must do what my gut tells me to do, because if it doesn't turn out how the book said it would, what will I do? Blame the book? As I write this I'm looking out my window and hear little birds chirping and a certain Bible verse comes to mind "Look at the birds of the air, that they do not sow, nor reap nor gather into barns, and yet your heavenly father feeds them. Are you not worth more than they? And who of you by being worried can add a single hour to his life?" Maybe we should be more like the birds and fly freely without the worry of what rules we should follow in love. We should trust that our counterpart is out there and when we meet him, he also won't feel a necessity to treat love like a game.

Needs

The shadow of my fingers
writing S's on his back.
The shadow of two bodies
moaning without clear sight.
He touches certain parts
you haven't touched in months.
He kisses certain areas
you forgot to love.
He rises to the moments
you lacked to care for.
Now I'm in the middle of positions
that as a woman I was yearning for.
Only problem is that it's with a man
I sadly do not love.
For you are the one I want
and my mind is solely constant for.
But still I let him finish
what I regretfully begun.
With the excuse that
we all have needs,
and one of them
unfortunately
is love.

People Aren't Games

People aren't games
You can't lose them
They simply make
The choice to leave.

What if?

What if I gave you leftovers of my love?
What if I made you feel so small?
What if I took my sun back?
What if I took my moon back?
What if I dropped down from each star?
And all I gave you was pride back.

What Is LOVE?

A friend suggested I write about the eternal question of whether a person can be in love with two people at the same time. Before I tackled that question, I decided to once again ask myself the same question I've asked since I was a teen: *What is love?* When I was a teen I asked myself what love was as if it was my duty to find an answer. Unbeknown to me that question would take me down a number of different paths, and without regret I learned from each one.

Everything I've learned about love makes me believe that one cannot be in love with two people at the same time or at least I can't. Why? Being *in love* and *loving* someone are two completely different things. Just how some people mistake the concepts of lust and love. Being in love is that craziness in the beginning of a relationship, those moments in which you feel you *need* to see that person, because you need to kiss him, and hug him and tell him how your vagina tingles for him. Okay, well you might not say that but that's how you feel! Then, that passionate feeling starts subsiding and that feeling turns into something familiarly bigger. Something unconditional, it turns into commitment, and in my opinion one cannot be committed to two different people. It's funny because many times people describe relationships as being 50/50. Two individuals who decide to meet half way. I believe a successful relationship is when both individuals give 100%. They give the relationship their all! The problem is that nowadays there are so many distractions, options, and people's ego interfering that it's almost impossible for two people to give 100% at the same time.

When I wrote *Letters, To The Men I Have Loved* I asked myself: *"When people part ways where does the love go?"* and I understood that loving someone did not necessarily mean **being in love.** "I Have Loved" is a PRESENT-PERFECT tense, meaning that what began in the past ended or continues in the present. I loved them then and I still love them now, but that doesn't mean I'm *in love with them today.* When you begin dating someone new it's important to cut ties with any exes, even while continuing to care for them. It's simple, if you continue giving the past energy it will be very hard for you to give quality energy to a new person in the present. I think that's the mistake some people make when they begin a new relationship. They carry on the baggage instead of starting from scratch, which leads them to feel confused and torn between two people. They begin to create a new emotional bond while still having an existing one with someone else.

When I observe my life today and how much I continue to grow, I realize I see love like beauty. The same way beauty is in the eye of the beholder, love is in the heart of the lover and it shouldn't be judged. Poets and philosophers throughout centuries have tried to find answers to the same question I have asked myself of "What is love?" They have all added their own piece of wisdom. Some will say it's respect, admiration, passion, giving, desire, kindness, commitment, willingness, and like any great mystery human beings will continue the pursuit of an answer. Because in the end, love is the most important pursuit of all, and it is the common thread that unites us.

What Is Romance?

Is romance another side dish of love?
One that is common among women
because of its lovely taste
that penetrates the buds of sentiments?

Is romance another fragrance?
One that cultivates the heart
with such delicate, and temperate soil
that enriches the soul.

Is romance the tender whisper beside one's ear?
Is it the song composed
by two fascinated hearts
inspired by an intense desire called love?

Is romance another simple joy?
Is it the joy of seeing
the naked eyes of who you love
and complimenting it with a caring look,
or is it the act of admiring a sensual figure?

Romance can be the taste of a kiss
or music played by two idealistic hearts
but beyond all the senses,

and all the passions,
romance is unexplainable
and only the heart retains the answer to this question.

Anchor on to your heart

My heart is beating
out of my chest.
Seeking you in a crowd full
Of dark haired men that aren't you.
My heart is beating
Out of my chest.
Brightly,
Strongly
Because it is in need
to anchor on to your heart.

Do We Need Reminders of Why We Love What We Love?

There's a moment when you realize what you want to do for the rest of your life, and if you're lucky you will love it. The problem is that careers are just like romantic relationships. It takes a lot of work to reach longevity. When I moved to Los Angeles I was very young and naïve. I was in love with acting, writing, and creating. Then one day like any relationship and its up and downs you think you might need to break up. "*The business of art*" diminished the love I had for my craft. Sometimes, disappointment hardens the heart, especially when innocence dies. My managers at the time motivated me to go back to class. I needed to learn to see my career with a different perspective and to see it with a new set of eyes. I signed up for the acting class my manager suggested and it was life-changing. I fell in love with acting all over again. I fell in love with the movies all over again.

As I meditated on a script I'm working on, I began to feel very nostalgic. I contemplated which steps to take next in different areas of my life, because the truth is that the journey of life will have bumps but one should never stop pursuing one's dreams. I decided to watch an Italian film I've loved for over a decade titled "Cinema Paradiso".

It is perhaps one of the best films I've ever watched. I can watch it over and over and never get tired of it. It is the story of a man named Salvatore during three very different stages of his life. First as a little boy in Sicily who falls in love with the movies, then as a teenager who falls in love for the first time with a girl named Elena, lastly as an older very successful film director returning to the small town that shaped him to meet once again all the ghosts from his past. Now this film is a tear-jerker, especially the much longer director's cut. As I was crying my big eyes out, I realized that my own memories of my first loves were very much alive. I began to think of when I was a teen I'd spend my afternoons watching old Hollywood movies, learning about things that people don't speak of anymore. How I would stay up for hours reading and discovering poets like Gustavo Adolfo Bécquer. How I spent hours painting and how I'd write little short films inspired by different experiences I had lived. All simply because I was in love with a world that I desperately wanted to be part of, *A Creative World.* When I met that expressive world, I changed. It broke my heart at times, so I never treated it the same way I did like those early years. I got married to it and stopped making to love it. Truthfully I began to treat it like a job unlike my first love. While I watched the film, I realized that just like everything else, we need reminders of why we love what we were born to love. Sometimes part of the job is to inject life into what's dying. The same way we can go to relationship counseling, or read books on how to fix our relationship, we should also do the same with all areas in our lives. We must breathe life into our passions before it's too late. We should never give up, and move on to the next like many do in this modern world we live in. As I watched "Cinema Paradiso" I saw the face of the young boy Salvatore as he experienced the movies for the very first time, how he'd get in trouble for spending all his time at the cinema, how he'd sneak in the cinema even when forbidden to go. It was watching a portrayal *love at first sight*-a person's first love developing, and it was contagious. So contagious that it served me as a reminder of how sad it would be if I allowed for my first passions to die and become faded memories.

The Creative Path

If you choose to follow a creative path,
then give in to your vulnerabilities.
Create what your heart gravitates to.
Don't think about what people will like or buy.
Create for your own personal need to express
and give voice to what keeps you up at night.
Create because that's your gift.
Create because it's in your DNA.
When criticism comes,
because there will always be criticism,
be absolutely proud of yourself
because you were authentic
and did it your way.

The Fascination

I'm fascinated by the universe
and unknown galaxies I'll never see.
The moon and her craters,
Perhaps the damage of untold secrets and dreams.
The planets and the mysticism behind their spins.
The stellar sky and the beauty
my hands will never grasp.
The challenge of seeking answers
for impossible questions.
I live in complete fascination constant desire to reconnect
All of my particles to the place where my soul was created.
That final place–
Where I know my soul belongs.

The Mantra

Pursue your passions
Accept your struggle
Let your pain shape you
And love transform you.

Are you READY?

It was May and wedding season. I was invited to a wedding at a breathtaking venue. The ceremony was very touching and meaningful because I've been friends with the couple for many years. As the bride walked in and arrived to meet the groom at the altar emotions came over me. She looked radiant, and with tears of joy the guests watched them become one under God. It was interesting because I've never been the girl to dream about a big wedding. Believe it or not I often say I would rather prefer to elope. The ceremony, which happened to be a Jewish wedding was romantic. The rabbi explained every part of their tradition and said something along the lines that the canopy where they were being married under was a Jewish tradition established during Moses' time. As soul mates they met under the symbolic canopy again in a different lifetime. As a romantic at heart I melted a little inside, and it had nothing to do with the Pasadena heat. I considered them to be lucky because so many people don't get to marry their true love, or even experience a true love. Not only did they meet, but now they were vowing to spend the rest of their life together, and that was beautiful.

After the ceremony we continued on to the reception, and as they had their first dance as husband

and wife I said to myself: "When your time comes you will not elope, you will commit in front of people. There is power in commitment. Your vows will be a poem. You will allow yourself this happiness." I've always believed in envisioning the things you want, but somehow I thought it was a somewhat un-organic to create vision boards for your personal life. That soon changed because I've come to realize that the energy we put out for our personal lives is just as important as what we put out in every other area. The idea that we have the power to manifest different desires should be celebrated, and not mocked with cynicism. I'm sure that if I were to ask the newlyweds if they always envisioned their wedding day, I can guarantee that they did. Maybe not as elaborate as the actual day, but they envisioned what they wanted and prioritized it.

Maybe I've prided myself in being too free and living the moment which is my nature, but that wedding reminded me I am still a woman of tradition, a woman who wants to marry the love of her life someday, and share that moment with her loved ones. Many people say marriage is just a paper, great for taxes, and a dying institution. Although, we are all entitled to our own opinion, I feel that marriage is still a meaningful example of commitment and love. Like the rabbi during the wedding said, it symbolizes a new beginning, just like a new moon. If that commitment will make you happier, sharpen your character and bring out the best in you, then envision it with someone who can inspire you to be your best version possible. In that moment I began to prepare my heart and began to envision a day like that for myself and because words are powerful I said: *One day it'll be me under a canopy committing to someone very special. Someone who will deserve all my love as well.*

Love Me

Love me for everything I'm not
But can become.
Love me beyond potential
Because in your eyes I am enough.
Love me without complications
Only with assurance
Love me in the sunlight
And accept me in my darkness.
Love me in my silence,
And when my eyes make love to you.
Love me for my thoughts,
And guard them in your vault.
Love me with transparency,
Where blurred lines do not abide.
Love me in my weakness,
Yet remind me of my strength.
Love me in the Spring
And collect my fallen leaves during the Autumn.
Love me as if my heart
Is your heart
And my feelings
Are your own.
Love me because
You enjoy loving me
It's beyond making love to me
Your soul has a need to love me
Because only I make you whole.

What is Your Vision of Love?

Many years ago an ex-boyfriend told me he considered my problem in relationships to be that I loved too hard. I told him I knew no other way than to love hard. The times I was given the chance at love I considered it a gift and I still do. Today I often ask myself: now that I'm more experienced with matters of the heart, will I love with the same fervor again? Will I give myself selflessly again? Because the truth is that after experiencing a number of heartbreaks something occurred to my heart, it became more guarded. My energy changed because deep inside I was tainted. I no longer was naïve to people's intentions with my heart. I learned that heartbreak occurs when too many expectations exist and unfortunately those expectations tarnish the idea of romantic love and shine light on the reality of love.

Thankfully my idealist nature has constantly provided me with hope of falling madly in love again and at times saved me from becoming cynical on the topic of love. Yet, to be an idealist is both a gift and a curse. We romanticize the small details, fantasize on moments not lived yet, and the infatuation takes us to such an exhilarating state that we convince ourselves that we are indeed in love. It can feel so good that many times I found myself chasing a feeling without thinking of the consequences. The excitement, the breathlessness, the desire, and the chemistry are powerful enough to blind anyone. To the point we will risk everything, after all the idea of love is the most intoxicating, powerful drug of all. Then one day we wake up from our trance and realize that those are only the symptoms of falling in love. Staying in love is a whole other ball game sometimes consisting of factors such as arguments, mistakes, disillusionments, compatibility, deception, and that's the hard part of love, the part we're never trained for but thankfully it's also the part that has made me wiser.

My parents have been married for thirty-eight years, which is considered a rarity in today's microwavable society. Of course many can assume they are probably used to each other and have a nice calm suburban life and the idea of separating would seem absurd and pointless. But no, they are still together because they truly love each other. When I was about twelve years old my mother passed out in the tub while taking a bath. When my dad found her he went into panic mode and began to scream and yell for one of my siblings or I to call 911. My mother was unconscious for a moment and although she was the one in an ill state, my father was on the floor appearing like he was dying in the brink of a heart attack. That day I learned that my father apart from being heavily dramatic, he could never live without my mother. His love for her ran so deep that their souls were entwined. Their commitment to each other was superior to any marital disagreement, financial tribulation, and beyond any fickle romantic idea of what we fantasize love to be. They aren't perfect but their example taught me that real love deals with high stakes and how much of your ego you can leave on the floor. Real love is about a personal decision to make an everyday effort to stay together for better or for worse, for rich or for poorer, in sickness and in health. Unfortunately, the reality is that many choose to check off the *irreconcilable differences* box once the excitement and the chemistry begins to fade. It's easier to give excuses as to why the love fizzled, than to admit you allowed it to fizzle. Because love is no different than anything else in life, it's always easier to quit than to persevere.

I'm still waiting for that type of love my father throughout the years has demonstrated my mother. I've looked within my own actions and realized I had to make certain changes in regards to the type of men I've given my love to in the past. Not because those men didn't love me because I know they did, but because some people love differently and I have my own vision of what love is. Perhaps my vision of love might seem outdated, and unrealistic to some, but for me it's that vision that has inspired me to keep me believing. It's the vision that has fueled me after every heartbreak and I shouldn't sacrifice that vision for another's ideology. When you have a vision you must align yourself with other people of similar vision. My mind tells me I need to be with a man who understands my vision of love, and my heart tells me someday he'll find me. I also recognize that outcome depends a lot on the men I choose to give quality time to and the effort I put into preparing myself to *receive* the type of love I want. Success in love much like in everything else is when preparation meets opportunity, sprinkled with a little luck of course. Luck we can't control, but like George Michael sang... *You gotta have faith.*

Sinatra Song

I've got you under my skin.
This is more than a Sinatra song.
I locked you in the deepest part of me.
Never did I think I could love so strong.
I'd do anything for you,
This is beyond dedicating songs.
But only this song can explain,
How you live under my skin,
How I have you concentrated in my blood.

It is necessary

It is necessary for me to have all of you.
Your mouth whenever I need it.
~~Your chest to sleep on every night,~~
Because the truth is,
your chest has always been my favorite pillow.

I Wonder

Sometimes I wonder
If when we finally meet
You'll know I was waiting
For you all along

Letters, To Women Like Me

Acknowledgements

To the women in my life, Thank you.
I am grateful for the sisterhood between us.
I am constantly inspired by you.
You all make me better.

About the Author

Mirtha Michelle Castro Mármol is a Dominican born actress and poet. She was raised in Miami, Florida. She wrote her first poem at the age of six, and since then she cultivated a passion for poetry. Mirtha Michelle is the author of the hugely popular, and best-selling poetry books *Letters, To The Men I Have Loved* and *Elusive Loves; Amores Esquivos.* With her books she has been able to capture the first feelings of love and loss in a raw form that has allowed her to earn the hearts of many loyal readers. She currently resides in Los Angeles, California.

CPSIA information can be obtained
at www.ICGtesting.com
Printed in the USA
BVOW06s1032180517
484499BV00015B/159/P